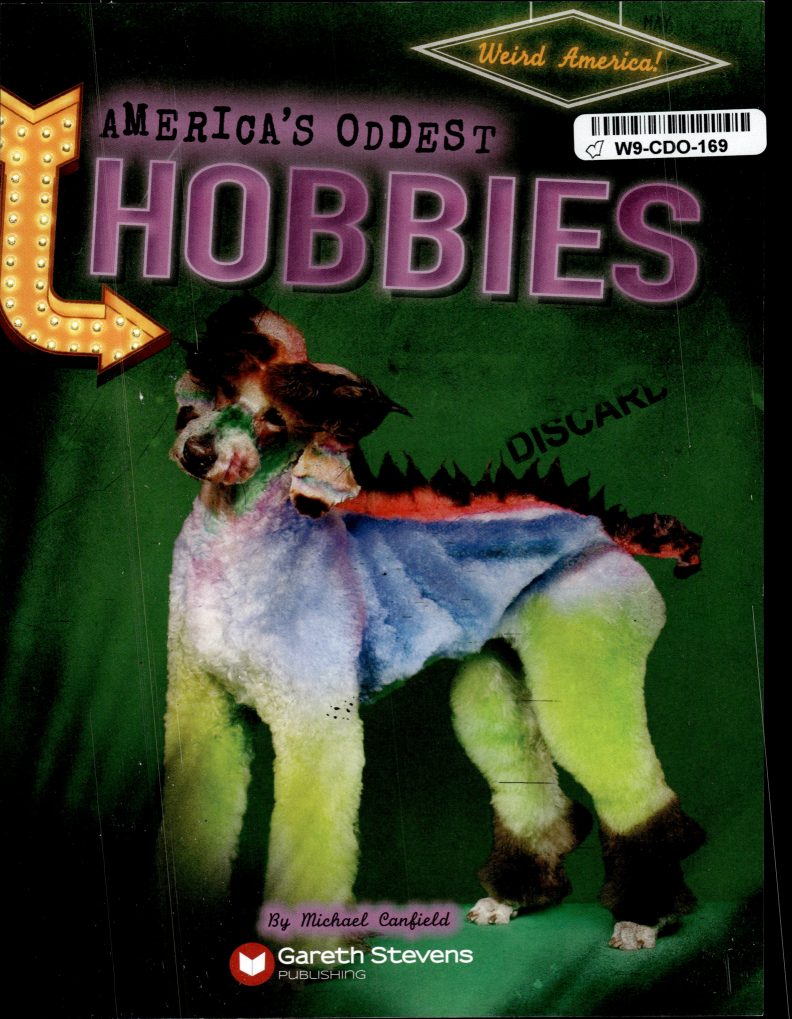

Weird America!

AMERICA'S ODDEST
HOBBIES

By Michael Canfield

Gareth Stevens
PUBLISHING

Please visit our website, www.garethstevens.com. For a free color catalog of all our high-quality books, call toll free 1-800-542-2595 or fax 1-877-542-2596.

Cataloging-in-Publication Data

Canfield, Michael T.
America's oddest hobbies / by Michael Thomas Canfield.
p. cm. — (Weird America)
Includes index.
ISBN 978-1-4824-4015-7 (pbk.)
ISBN 978-1-4824-4016-4 (6-pack)
ISBN 978-1-4824-4017-1 (library binding)
1. Hobbies — Juvenile literature. 2. Hobbies — Miscellanea — Juvenile literature. I. Canfield, Michael, 1977-. II. Title.
GV1201.C36 2016
790.13—d23

First Edition

Published in 2016 by
Gareth Stevens Publishing
111 East 14th Street, Suite 349
New York, NY 10003

Copyright © 2016 Gareth Stevens Publishing

Designer: Sarah Liddell
Editor: Ryan Nagelhout

Photo credits: Cover, p. 1 (arrow) Mascha Tace/Shutterstock.com; cover, pp. 1 (main), 6, 7, 8, 9 Barcroft/Contributor/ Barcroft Media/Getty Images; sidebar used throughout zayats-and-zayats/Shutterstock.com; background texture used throughout multipear/Shutterstock.com; p. 4 Gunner Pippel/Shutterstock.com; p. 5 Maria Dryfhout/Shutterstock.com; p. 10 blackboard1965/Shutterstock.com; p. 11 (cones) liam1949/Shutterstock.com; p. 11 (hawaiian shirts) Matthew Cole/Shutterstock.com; p. 11 (metal back scratcher) Moolkum/Shutterstock.com; p. 11 (wooden back scratcher) nito/ Shutterstock.com; p. 11 (green back scratcher) Prapann/Shutterstock.com; p. 11 (metal pencil sharpener) Barry Blackburn/Shutterstock.com; p. 11 (red pencil sharpener) WitthayaP/Shutterstock.com; p. 11 (blue pencil sharpener) Nika Novak/Shutterstock.com; p. 11 (fortunes) FlickrLickr/Wikimedia Commons; p. 12 Eric Isselee/Shutterstock.com; p. 13 Alfred Eisenstaedt/Contributor/The LIFE Picture Collection/Getty Images; p. 14 Michael Fairchild/Photolibrary/ Getty Images; p. 15 Quigley/Wikimedia Commons; p. 16 (baseball) Dan Thornberg/Shutterstock.com; p. 16 (paint can) Nils Z/Shutterstock.com; p. 17 Bob Croslin/Contributor/Sports Illustrated/Getty Images; p. 18 Palnatoke/ Wikimedia Commons; p. 19 Robert Lackenbach/Contributor/The LIFE Images Collection/Getty Images; p. 20 Buyenlarge/Contributor/Archive Photos/Getty Images; p. 21 Jonathunder/Wikimedia Commons; p. 23 Kevin Zen/ Contributor/Getty Images News/Getty Images; p. 24 Keystone/Hulton Archive/Getty Images; p. 25 Kent Kobersteen/ National Geographic Magazines/Getty Images; p. 27 (sign) David Muir/Photographer's Choice/Getty Images; p. 27 (main) Andrew Rich/Vetta/Getty Images; p. 28 Brian Kinney/Shutterstock.com; p. 29 STAN HONDA/Staff/AFP/ Getty Images.

Printed in the United States of America

CPSIA compliance information: Batch #CW16GS: For further information contact Gareth Stevens, New York, New York at 1-800-542-2595.

CONTENTS

Words in the glossary appear in **bold** type the first time they are used in the text.

WEIRD HOBBIES!

Hobbies are activities we take part in on a regular basis for fun. They include doing things, making things, and even collecting things. Americans love their hobbies, from stamp collecting and building models to beekeeping!

We get to choose our hobbies, unlike other activities we have to do like cleaning our room or homework. While most people's hobbies are common—like collecting baseball cards—some people like to explore the weird side of life. Let's take a look at some of the oddest things people do for hobbies!

What's Your Hobby?

Everyone has a hobby, even if you've never thought about it before. Some people like to play sports or take part in outdoor activities like hiking or kayaking. Others like to read or collect things, like seashells. What do you like to do in your free time?

Stamp collecting is just one of many hobbies considered "ordinary" in society.

EXTREME DOG GROOMING

Is that a lion or a dog? It's a question you might find yourself asking if you go to an **extreme** dog **grooming** show. Extreme dog grooming shows are much different from regular dog shows, where dogs are judged on a set of standards based on their breed. In extreme grooming shows—called competitions—creativity is key. Dog owners spend hundreds of dollars to make their pooch look like another animal or even an entire scene!

Dogs have even been turned into movie characters like Yoda from *Star Wars*! One dog made up to look like Yoda had an Ewok on his behind!

Dogs have their fur shaped into all kinds of different things—even train cars!

Best in Show

Some types of dogs are better for extreme grooming than others. Poodles are popular because their fur is very fluffy and can easily be made to look like other animals. Many grooming shops specialize in turning furry friends into extreme animals.

Getting a dog ready for an extreme grooming show can take days! Through the grooming process, the dog's fur is cut and shaped to look like whatever their owner chooses. Nontoxic dyes are added to a dog's fur over the course of a few days. This helps the fur get to be the right color and creates patterns that can take home the top prize. Some contests give out $5,000 to the winning pooch and its owner.

Is It Cruel?

Some people question whether dyeing a dog's fur and grooming them to look like other animals is a **cruel** way of handling our furry friends. But dog owners and extreme groomers say they try to make the dogs comfortable. They argue the dogs are pampered, or treated better than most dogs!

SAM

Are dogs in extreme grooming competitions treated fairly? What do you think about this odd hobby?

TOENAIL COLLECTING

A Louisiana man has been collecting his toenail and fingernail clippings for decades! Richard Gibson figures he has thousands of nail clippings in a big jar he keeps at home. He started in 1978, placing them at first in a **manicure** kit box before moving to the jar when the box was filled.

Gibson keeps his nails long, only cutting them when they break. He keeps the jar on a shelf in his home and said he started collecting the nails just to see how long it would take to fill the first box. More than 35 years later, he's still collecting!

What's Next?

Gibson submitted his own nail collection to the fact book *Ripley's Believe It or Not.* He's actually sent 70,000 different weird facts to Ripley's newspaper column. Gibson says his jar is almost full and he doesn't know what he'll do when there's no room for new nail clippings.

ODD AMERICAN COLLECTIONS

back scratchers

traffic cones

pencil sharpeners

hawaiian shirts

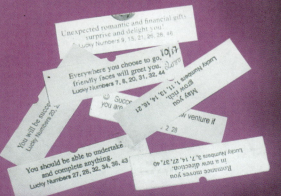

fortune cookie fortunes

11

MOOING

The Moo-la-palooza is a yearly contest held at the Wisconsin State Fair. **Contestants** compete to see who can moo like a cow the best. Contestants range in age from children to adults, and the best "moo-er" wins $1,000 in free sandwiches for a year, a cow-print jacket, and a golden cowbell. Judges for the event look for realism, style, and originality in contestants' moos.

Participants in the contest practice all year for the event. The moo-ers say it's fun and enjoy showing off their talents in front of a big crowd. How would you do in a mooing contest?

Boy Wins Moo-la-palooza

Ten-year-old Austin Siok won Moo-la-palooza at the Wisconsin State Fair in 2010. After Siok won the contest, people asked him to moo wherever he went, including at the bank and in stores! Siok, who didn't grow up on a farm, said the win made him feel like he was famous.

Other groups have held mooing contests at fairs and parties for years. Anna McGinnis, below, won a mooing contest at Hidden Valley Farm in the 1950s!

GLADIATOR BUGS

One strange hobby involves having different insects fight. Called **Gladiator** Bugs, the hobby started in Japan. Insects are placed in a small box and battle each other. Tarantulas battle scorpions, praying mantises fight beetles, and hornets fight centipedes. Each bug has its strengths and weaknesses, and people love testing their bugs to see which ones are better fighters.

Insect breeders will train their bugs and give them high-energy foods, like sugar, before a fight. Insect fighting is popular in many other Asian countries. Some people even bet money on the fights!

Fighting Crickets

Having crickets fight each other has been a pastime in China for centuries. Unlike other bug battles, cricket fighting rarely leads to injuries for the insects. It was outlawed in China for a few decades, but it's recently made a comeback among younger people and is very popular online.

Schoolchildren sometimes make bugs fight each other in milk jugs.

15

BASEBALLS AND PAINT

In 1977, Indiana native Michael Carmichael decided to have his 3-year-old son paint a baseball. Decades later, the baseball has received more than 24,500 coats of paint and weighs at least 5,000 pounds (2,268 kg)!

The ball is now so big, it requires several steel rods to hang from the roof of the special house it's in. Carmichael even lets other people add a new coat of paint to the baseball. There's only one rule—whatever color you add has to be different from the color already on the ball.

Early Start

Carmichael first played around with a baseball and paint while playing the sport in 1966. A baseball fell into some paint, and the young ballplayer wondered how much paint he could add. Carmichael dipped the ball in paint and added coats for the next 2 years until it was the size of a football.

The McKenney family of Florida are big fans of the Tampa Bay Rays. They have collected the signatures of every Rays player and coach on baseballs!

TREE SHAPING

Tree shapers create art out of living trees. These artists use trees and shrubs to make living sculptures, mirrors, chairs, and even footbridges.

There are several different ways to shape plants into art. Sometimes **saplings** are encouraged to grow into a certain form over several years. Other times, older trees are bent into place until they grow that way. Either way, tree shaping takes a long time! It may take up to a decade to finish a chair design! The practice has been around for hundreds of years, and some people even make a living shaping trees for customers today!

Erlandson's Cube Tree

Erlandson's Tree Circus

Young Axel Erlandson came to America from Sweden in the 1880s with his parents. He started tree shaping in California in the 1920s and created a farm full of weird tree creations he called the Tree Circus. When children asked how he shaped the trees, Erlandson replied, "Oh, I talk to them."

Erlandson sold the Tree Circus before his death in 1964.

19

CUTTING THE MUSTARD

Late one night in a grocery store in 1986, a voice told a lawyer named Barry Levenson to start collecting mustard. He bought about a dozen jars that night, and today Levenson owns the world's largest collection of mustard jars. Levenson soon left his job with the state of Wisconsin to start the National Mustard Museum. More than 5,600 samples are on display in Middleton, Wisconsin.

Levenson has a mustard from every state and more than 70 countries! He uses special gloves to handle his collection, which includes old mustard tins, glass jars, and even old ads for mustards.

some of Levenson's mustard jars

All Mustard, All the Time

Levenson really loves mustard. He only wears yellow clothing, matching the color of mustard. He also puts mustard on all kinds of foods, including sweets like cake. Levenson uses mustard instead of shaving cream! In 1987, he even argued a big court case with a small jar of mustard in his pocket!

CARVING EGGSHELLS

Coloring eggs is a tradition in a lot of places, but what about carving eggshells? That's just what Iowa native Gary LeMaster does, creating amazing works of art out of the shells we usually throw away.

LeMaster grew up using woodworking tools and with a love of fine arts. He uses chicken, turkey, and ostrich eggs that have failed to hatch and carefully cleans them out. Using a pencil, he traces an outline on the egg and uses tools made for diamond cutting to create the works.

What Is That?

Although LeMaster's artworks are shaped like eggs, most people don't believe they're real eggshells because of how cool they look. Instead, plastic or **ceramic** seem more likely to people, LeMaster says, but he assures them that they're real eggshells. In fact, LeMaster started an eggshell-carving magazine to teach people about his **unique** hobby!

Other artists around the world actually carve on eggshells, too!

ALL ABOARD!

Do you like trains? Some people like them so much their hobby is watching them go by! These people are called train spotters, and they often "collect" the number that's on the train as it passes. Most collectors simply look for the number of the train engine, but some go so far as to collect the numbers on the train cars themselves.

When train spotters meet to watch for trains, they often make it a social event, bringing along sandwiches. The hobby reached its peak after World War II and has died down in recent years due to the lack of trains used for **transportation**.

early train spotters

Planes, Trains, and Automobiles

Trains aren't the only mode of transportation people like to watch. There are people who enjoy looking at different cars and airplanes as well. In fact, there are online groups where people share their pictures and videos of trains, cars, and planes.

Locomotives like the one pictured are no longer in service in the United States. This means there are fewer trains to spot!

CRYPTOZOOLOGY

Have you heard of Bigfoot? What about the Abominable Snowman? For some people, looking for these creatures that may or may not exist is a hobby. People who do this are called cryptozoologists, and they spend time and money searching for "cryptids," animals that may not exist.

Cryptozoology isn't a science, because it's based largely on stories and myths, not proof or facts. Those who spend their time searching for ape-men or sea monsters love the idea of being the first to discover something we don't know exists.

Is That Real?

Many pictures and videos of "Bigfoot"—also called "Sasquatch"—have emerged over the years, only to be set aside as fakes. Bigfoot hunters say they've found footprints and other physical evidence that the large, mythical creature exists. These cryptozoologists say they've recorded Bigfoot calls in the wild and spend their free time searching the woods in various forests throughout the United States. What do you think? Is Bigfoot real?

Despite this Sasquatch Crossing sign, there is no proof the large beast exists. Nonetheless, there's even a Bigfoot Trail in California named for it!

SASQUATCH CROSSING

WHAT'S YOUR HOBBY?

You don't have to collect toenails or go searching for Bigfoot to have a hobby. In fact, you probably already have a hobby, even if you don't think of it as such. Do you play video games, read, or play a sport? Yes? Then you have a hobby!

But is your hobby... weird? The people mentioned in this book probably don't think their hobby is unusual. Maybe weird is just something we're not familiar with. So whether you're searching for Bigfoot or playing a musical instrument, embrace your hobby. You never know where it'll take you!

All Kinds of Weird

Other strange American hobbies include a man who likes to photograph himself playing dead and another who travels the country and tries to be in the background of live television news shots. Some people travel all over the country to ride different roller coasters. Now that's a fun hobby!

Many people spend years trying to grow the largest fruits or vegetables to win contests and ribbons.

GLOSSARY

ceramic: matter shaped into a figure and heated to harden

contestant: a person who takes part in a contest

cruel: causing harm or suffering to others

extreme: existing to a very great degree

gladiator: a fierce fighter

groom: to make neat and attractive

locomotive: an engine that moves under its own power

manicure: a beauty treatment for one's hands, usually focused on the nails

sapling: a young tree

transportation: the act or process of moving something from one place to another

unique: unusual or special

FOR MORE INFORMATION

BOOKS

Beaver, Simon. *Sport, Game, or Hobby?* New York, NY: Cambridge University Press, 2013.

Wilson, Jacqueline. *Hobby Journal.* London, United Kingdom: Doubleday Children's Books, 2014.

WEBSITES

The Carving Process
theeggshellsculptor.com/the-carving-process/
Learn more about how to carve eggshells from Gary LeMaster.

Dog Grooming Competition—in Pictures
theguardian.com/lifeandstyle/gallery/2013/jun/18/
dog-grooming-competition-in-pictures
Check out some of the crazy designs on these competition dogs.

The Train Spotter Guide
tripbase.com/c/trainspotting
Find out more about train spotting and its history here.

INDEX